Angels, Angels, Angels

EDITH P. LAZENBY

authorHOUSE®

AuthorHouse™
1663 Liberty Drive
Bloomington, IN 47403
www.authorhouse.com
Phone: 1-800-839-8640

Published by AuthorHouse 12/03/2014

ISBN: 978-1-4969-5608-8 (sc)
ISBN: 978-1-4969-5607-1 (e)

Contents

~Dedication~

This book is dedicated to my mother and father, Walter and Marjorie Lazenby who I now believe is one of the good angels rejoicing in heaven with the Lord, and assigned to watch over me. I love you mom and dad, but God loved you better.

~❧Introduction❧~

Have you ever put something down in a place and when you went back to retrieve it, it wasn't there? So you question your sanity knowing good and well you placed that certain item in that particular place, but now you can't find it. After searching everywhere you decide to look one more time where you thought you had placed the item and behold, there it is. How could this be?

Have you ever been somewhere and it felt like someone touched your hair and when you looked around no one was there? This happens from time to time, angels letting you know in their own way they are present. So do you or do you not believe in angels?

Whenever we turn the television on or go to the movies or even rent DVD's we see depictions of angels as demons, evil, invading, destructive and doing every evil thing imaginable. There was a television show once called "Touched by an Angel." It show the kindness of God, and it showed the angels giving people warnings, and it also showed the dark side of angels, where death was portrayed as an angel. So we ask ourselves, do angels really exist? Are there really good angels that protect us and bad angels that want to destroy us? For answers to these and other questions we must go to the greatest book ever written and that is the Bible, God's Word.

Revelation 1:1 establishes the fact that angels are messengers of God because verse one states:

> "The revelation of Jesus Christ, which God gave unto him, to shew unto his servants things which must come to pass: and he sent and signified it by his angel unto his servant John."

Obviously since we are unable to see angelic beings with the natural eye we dismiss the idea angels are real. God's Word the Bible was put here to give us warning about things we are faced with, and the consequences that happen to us if we fail to heed his Word. We either don't believe that the Bible is God's Word, or we don't care if it's God's Word. We want to do our own thing because we only live once. True, we only live once and then the judgment.

We all laughed at one time or another about going to hell and party with all our friends that are going to be there. But, one day reality set in because we heard someone talk about a man called Jesus. A spark started with us, which in turn made us inquisitive about the Bible. When we picked up this awesome book and decided to read it we were astonished at the priceless information it held. It told us about angels. Angelic beings that served God in heaven and constantly praised God day and night saying Holy, Holy, Holy is the Lord God Almighty.

Then we read about another angel that had been created by God. The Bible describes him as the most beautiful angel ever created and his name was Lucifer, also known as "Son of the Morning." One day pride took over Lucifer and he decided, I want to be worshipped like God. I want to be God.

There are still two thirds of the angels God created in heaven serving God, watching over his children, protecting them and what ever else angles are assigned to do. However, there are one third of the angels along with their leader cast out of heaven, now wrecking havoc among the children of God here on earth, because their domain includes the air, ground and sea. But one day as we see depicted in the movies, the good will overcome evil, and Jesus will come back for his people.

⟶✦Angels✦⟵

Since there is a misconception today that demons are not real so they should not be classified as angels. Because of this error in teaching, people do not believe in demons. They have been down played to appear as beings with two horns, dressed in a red suit, having a tale and/or pitchfork. But, beloved we have been lulled into thinking the drawings we have seen in books, on wall paintings, in museums, and elsewhere that depict angels only as small babies (cherubim's), or half clothed adults with or without wings flying around or hovering over individuals are the only angels that exist; when in actuality we have and are being deceived.

Let's get real and look at what and who angels really are. There are good angels who were created by God because the Word of God states, "all things were made by him; and without him was not anything made that was made" (John 1:3). Then we have some evil angels that were once good, but decided to follow in the footsteps of Lucifer, whose name means brightness[1] and is also known as the Son of the Morning, who rebelled against God because he wanted to be God. The Bible says God will not share his glory with another (Isaiah 42:8), and that goes for beings He has created whether in heaven or in earth. Lucifer and one third of the angels who were on Lucifer's side was expelled from heaven, and some are chained in hell, awaiting the tribulation period to be loosed, some are wrecking havoc in people's lives who refuse to live for God, and others have assignments over territories, countries, cities, neighborhoods, blocks, homes and what have you.

In reality demons are fallen angels that once held some sort of position in heaven, serving God until Lucifer, decided to usurp his authority and overthrow God and become God (Isaiah 14:12-15). After Lucifer, defected and was removed from heaven (Revelation 12:9), his name was changed to Satan which means deceiver. He now walks about seeking whom he may devour. His main purpose is to steal, to kill, and to destroy, anyone that names the name of Jesus.

---

[1] Merrill F. Unger, Unger's Bible Dictionary, (Chicago, Moody Press, 1983), p.670.

So with all that do angels really exist? If so, are there good angels or are there nothing but bad angels? These are some fascinating questions. So where does one go to find the answer; to Webster's dictionary, or maybe the Encyclopedia Britannica, or maybe even to the New World Encyclopedia. These books will give you the definition of angels, but these books are not going to give you the answers you are looking for. The best book to go to learn about angels is the Bible.

Oh sure, many have said the Bible is full of errors, but on closer examination you will find the Bible is the only book that tells it like it is, and can prove what is written is the truth. So where do we find angels in the Bible, because I thought it was full of fables. To answer this statement you find angels written about in the Old and New Testaments of the Bible. In the Old Testament the Hebrew word for angels is "MALAK" in the New Testament the Greek word is "ANGELOS."[2] When translated both words means "Ambassador or Messenger." It is also used to mean guardian or representative as found in Revelation 1:20 which states:

---

[2] <u>Unger</u>, Bible Dictionary, p,52.

"The mystery of the seven stars which thou sawest in my right hand, and the seven golden candlesticks. The seven stars are the angels of the seven churches, and the seven candlesticks which thou sawest are the seven churches."

and Matthew 18:10

"Take heed that ye despise not one of these little ones; for I say unto you, that in heaven their angels do always behold the face of my Father which is in heaven."

and Acts 12:15

"And they said unto her, thou are mad, But she constantly affirmed that it was even so. Then said they, It is his angel."

So we see that angels are beings created by God to serve as messengers or ambassadors for the Word states:

"For by him were all things created, that are in heaven, and that are in earth, visible and invisible, whether they be thrones, or dominions, or principalities, or powers: all things were created by him, and for him:" (Corinthians 1:16).

Angels are superior to man because Psalm 8:4-5 states:

"What is man, that thou are mindful of him? and the son of man, that thou visitest him? For thou hast madest him a little lower than the angels, and crowned him with glory and honour."

We first read about angels in the book of Genesis, which means "beginning" when God placed cherubim's, which are angels at the "east of the garden of Eden to keep man from reentering the garden of Eden and eating from the tree of life." Genesis 3:24 states:

"So he drove out the man; and he placed at the east of the garden of Eden Cherubims, and a flaming sword which turned every way, to keep the way of the tree of life."

When you first read this you should wonder why was it necessary for man to be expelled from the Garden of Eden. When you look at the consequences of disobedience to God's simple commandment of not eating from the tree of good and evil, just the word evil should have sent off a warning in Adam's mind that something awful could happen if he disobeyed. But such is mankind. Curiosity costs us unnecessary grief when we knowingly do something wrong as in the case of Adam and Eve; they brought about sin into the world which has brought about death and disease.

As stated before Angels in the New Testament means "angelos: or ambassador or "messenger."

> "And of the angels he saith who maketh his angels spirits, and his ministers, aflame of fire:" (Hebrews 1:7),

> and

> "Are they not all ministering spirits, sent forth to minister for them who shall be heirs of salvation" (Hebrews 1:14).

God has made the angels superior to man. Why is this? Well, scripture states, "for thou hast made him (speaking of man) a little lower than the angels and hath crowned him with glory and honor" (Psalm 8:5; Hebrews 2:8). If angels and man were on the same level they would not be able to minister the things God has shown them to protect, provide, and deliver God's people in time of need.

As we look back in history, the history of the Bible, we will note that all angels were created by God and for God. One must wonder how did one angel named Lucifer, which means Son of the Morning, the most beautiful angel in heaven let his beauty and ego, also known as pride get the best of him, whereby he decided he wanted to be God. He wanted to be worshipped, he wanted to be in charge failing to realize that he was created by God to serve God.

> "How are thou fallen from heaven, O Lucifer, son of the morning"...
> For thou has said in thine heart, I will exalt my throne above the stars of God: I will sit also upon the mount of the congregation, in the sides of the north. I will ascend above the heights of the clouds: I will be like the most high" (Isaiah 14:12-14).

Lucifer, now known as Satan was not satisfied being in the state he was in. He wanted to be worshipped. Let's look a moment at mankind. The Bible which we know is the Word of God, tells us that pride comes before a fall. We don't have to be in any important position to become prideful. Someone could give you a compliment about how good you look, or you might be promoted on your job as someone in a supervisory position and these things might cause you to become puffed up. You might even serve the Lord in a pastoral position and forget you are to shepherd the sheep, not become demanding and controlling over the sheep that has been placed under your care.

So many of us who have been placed in authority become puffed up, forgetting where they have come from. So many people who get saved and work in the church or hold an office in the church forget where they came from, what God delivered them from and how to be nice to people. They get puffed up just like Satan and want to be in control.

> "I am the Lord: that is my name: and my glory will I not give to another, neither my praise to graven images" (Isaiah 42:8).

The angels were given a free mind to choose whom they would serve, just as man has been given a free mind to choose whom they will serve. Even though mankind is born into this world in sin (Psalm 51:5), and sin separates him from God, and Satan is his master, when mankind reaches the age of accountability he or she must make a decision to whom they owe their allegiance, God the creator of all or to Satan the devil. What is the age of accountability? The Word of God does not specify an answer to this, but what we know is that when a person reaches an age where they are able to tell right from wrong, they are accountable for their actions. The Bible exhorts parents to;

> "train up a child in the way he should go: and when he is old, he will not depart from it" (Proverbs 22:8),

Also the Word of God states;

> "He that spareth his rod hateth his son: but he that loveth him chasten him betimes" (Proverbs 13:24).

In other words if you fail to discipline a child then they figure whatever they do is right, because no correction was given to correct them.

Unfortunately Lucifer decided he wanted to be God, and since he rebelled in heaven, there was no place for two rulers to exist. When Lucifer tried to overthrow the kingdom of God, he found out God would not tolerate his behavior and banished him from heaven, one third of the angels decided to be on Lucifer's side, and they were also cast out of heaven along with Lucifer.

> "And there was war in heaven: Michael and his angels fought against the dragon; and the dragon fought and his angels, and prevailed not; neither was their place found any more in heaven. And the great dragon was cast out, that old serpent, called the Devil, and Satan, which deceiveth the whole world: he was cast out into the earth, and his angels were cast out with him" (Revelation 12:7-9).

Lucifer whose name was now changed to Satan, was cast out of heaven (Luke 10:8), and now roam the earth seeking whom he may devour (1Peter 5:8). It must be noted not all the angels rebelled and revolted with Lucifer. It was one third of the angels that followed Satan to earth. A few were cast into hell and are in chains waiting the time of tribulation where they will be loosed from the bottomless pit (Revelation 12:9). Satan and his angels became the prince of this world and he has been deceiving people ever since he deceived Eve in the Garden of Eden. No one is immune to Satan's deception. He even tried to deceive Jesus who was before Satan and knew his deceitful ways.

As Christians we must rely on the Word of God, because it is the Word of God that is going to keep us. When Satan tried to deceive and tempt Jesus he used the Word against him, "It is written." Three powerful words we need to be aware of and use against Satan when he tries to deceive us. We sometimes wonder why at times we feel aches and pains in our bodies, or why we often get tired, or why we get depressed, or the many other things or obstacles we encounter. This is because:

> "We wrestle not against flesh and blood, but against principalities, against powers, against the rulers of the darkness of this world, against spiritual wickedness in high places" (Ephesians 6:12).

We cannot see demons with our natural eyes but they are real. Very seldom do you hear anyone teach or preach on demons which these fallen angels are now called. Whether we want to admit it demons are real just as angels are real. We often wonder why some people act the way they do. Could it be they are under the influence of demons?

I believe we are oppressed by Satan because that is his job. People are oppressed and possessed by demons who are without Christ in their lives. A lot of the sickness we have today come from the devil himself even though people blame God for their sickness. Let's look at the Word of God and see what it has to say.

> "And if a kingdom be divided against itself, that kingdom cannot stand:" (Mark 3:24).

> "He sent His word, and healed them, and delivereth them from their destructions" (Psalm 107:20).

> "But he was wounded for our transgressions, he was bruised for our iniquities: the chastisement of our peace was upon him; and with his stripes we are healed" (Isaiah 53:5).

God speaking to Satan;

"Hast thou considered my servant Job, that there is none like him in the earth, a perfect and an upright man, one that feareth God, and escheweth (hateth) evil" (Job 1:8).

"And the Lord said unto Satan, Behold, all that he hath is in thy power; only upon himself put not forth thine hand. So Satan went forth from the presence of the Lord" (Job 1:12).

"The thief cometh not, but for to steal, and to kill, and to destroy: I am (Jesus) come that they (we) might have life, and that they might have it more abundantly" (John 10:10).

"Beloved, I wish above all things that thou mayest prosper and be in health, even as thou soul prospereth" (3 John 2).

So as we look at these few scriptures we see it is not God, but Satan who puts sickness on us and then plants the notion or idea that it was God who made you sick, or disabled. Some types of illness are generational. That is why it is so important to know your family tree history. This is why when you go to the doctor the first thing they want to know is your family history. Who in your family had heart problems, diabetes, headaches, eye problems, and the list goes on.

Again we turn to the Word of God and to both the Old and New Testaments. In the Book of Deuteronomy God says, "if you will obey my commandments I will let none of these diseases come upon you" (Exodus 15:26). The clue here is if you will "obey." Once you refuse to obey the commandments of God then you open yourself up to the wiles of the devil. You are not under the protection of God. Then if you obey God he will protect you from these attacks of Satan.

But beloved, the Bible tells us that it rains on the just as well as the unjust. The Bible also tells us, "if we suffer, we shall also rein with him; if we deny him, he also will deny us" (2 Timothy 2:12). Additionally, because of sin we will all suffer with something before we leave this world. How can I say this? Well, just as it rains on the just it will also rain on the unjust. When Jesus was here in the flesh he dealt with numerous types of infirmities. One in particular is a woman who was bound. She could not walk up straight. She was bent over in half. "And ought not this woman, being a daughter of Abraham, whom Satan hath bound, lo, these eighteen years, be loosed from this bond on the Sabbath day? (Luke 13:16). This scripture clearly shows how the devil who is no respecter of persons had afflicted this woman, and she was unable to stand up straight. Satan showed this woman no compassion, and believe it or not he is not going to show you any compassion. He doesn't care about you. His job is to steal, kill and to destroy. Steal your joy, your family, your faith, and to kill your desire to do things.

Not only that he desires to destroy you. He doesn't want to see you succeed in anything you do. There was a woman with an issue of blood for 12 long years (Mark 5:25; Luke 8:43). According to the Levitical law she was unclean. She was an outcast. She went to the doctors, spent all she had trying to get well, but the doctors could not help her. Put yourself in her place. No friends, an outcast, no chance or opportunity to meet a future husband, no chance of having children, unable to associate with your family because they will probably make fun or ridicule you. You wonder why is this happening to me? Why is God letting this happen? When we look back through scripture we find out some things are handed down through generations. This means we inherit certain things in life. Is this fair? We could say no this is not fair, so we need to find out how we can change the situation, who can we turn too?

The woman with the issue of blood heard about a man called Jesus who was going around healing the sick, raising the dead, casting out demons, and feeding the hungry. Through hearing about Jesus her faith raised within her, and she said "if I may touch the hem of his garment, I will be made whole" (Mark 5:28). Her faith rose up within her. If I can just touch – that's all it took was faith. The Bible says, "Now faith." We all have a measure of faith. We just have to exercise it in all situations and refuse to doubt. Yes, Satan will bring doubt to your mind, but you must learn how to bind up doubt and loose your faith.

~Types of Demonic Angels~

The angels of Satan otherwise known as demons comes in various forms such as <u>lying spirits;</u>

> "And the Lord said unto him, Wherewith? And he said I will go forth, and I will be a lying spirit in the mouth of all his prophets. And he said, thou shalt persuade him and prevail also; go forth, and do so" (1 Kings 22:22).

The example we could use here is a child since we are all born in sin through our Adamic nature. A child is a very curious individual, learning about how things work, experimenting with things, touching things and if you ask them a question the first thing they will do is tell a lie. Did you break the lamp? No one else was around and all evidence point to the child, but instead of telling the truth the child will tell a lie. Because of sin, unknowingly a lying spirit used the child to tell the untruth. We have to be very careful when someone prophesies to you about things, because everyone that says they are a prophet is not a prophet of God, but of Satan. A true prophet will confirm what you already know to be true. A true prophet from God does not tear down and instill fear in you. They confirm to you what God has already told you. We must remember that Satan is a liar and the father of lies.

Seducing spirits,

> "Now the spirit speaketh expressly, that in the latter times, some shall depart from the faith, giving heed to seducing spirits and doctrines of devils" (1 Timothy 4:1).

It is so easy to be seduced today with all the drugs, alcohol, pornography, displays of nakedness, lewd dancing, and other enticing material available to you via the internet, adult toy shops, and magazine displays if you are not a strong person. It's easy to be seduced if you are having marital problems, because you might listen to a lying spirit other than the voice of God telling you it's okay to go and have a little fun. Having a little fun sometime causes grave consequences such as disease, breakup of your marriage, and other regrettable things. You can be seduced if you set yourself up to entertain a seducing spirit because of your unfaithfulness. Believe me this spirit will not come out and tell you if you play with fire you will get burnt.

> Foul spirits,

>> "when Jesus saw that the people were running together, he rebuked the foul spirit" (Mark 9:25).

>> "And he cried mightily with a strong voice, saying, Babylon the great is fallen, is fallen, and is become the habitation of devils, and the hold of every foul spirit, and a cage of every unclean and hateful bird" (Revelation 18:2).

In Mark 9:25 Jesus rebuked the foul spirit, and cast out the deaf and dumb spirit that had inhibited the young boy. It should be noted Jesus asked the father, "how long is it ago since this came unto him?" and the father answered Jesus, "of a child." Some way a door was opened by the child or parent for the demon to enter into him. We do not know what door was opened but we do know by the child's action he was demon possessed, but thanks be to God, Jesus cast the demon out of the child.

During the tribulation period every demonic spirit will be unleashed upon the world. Right now some are restrained in hell in chains to be released by God upon an unrighteous world. We have not seen the havoc that Satan can and will unleash upon the world, because he will come against the children of God and every immoral thing imaginable will take place.

Deaf and dumb spirits,

> "And when the devil was cast out, the dumb spake: and the multitudes marveled saying. it was never so seen in Israel:" (Matthew 9:33).

and

> "thou dumb and deaf spirit, I charge thee, come out of him, and enter no more into him" (Mark 9:25b).

This is just an example that God does not put sickness or infirmities upon a person. For a person to have a deaf and dumb spirit inhabiting him or her, this would either be a generational curse, a promise by someone prior to the child's birth to dedicate the child to the devil or a door was opened somewhere along the line for this demon to enter and take up residence.

Deceiving spirits,

"For there are many unruly and vain talkers and deceivers, specially they of the circumcision" (Titus 1:10).

"But evil men and seducers shall wax worse and worse, deceiving, and being deceived" (2 Timothy 3:13).

"And the kings of the earth, who have committed fornication and lived deliciously with her, shall bewail her, and lament for her, when they shall see the smoke of her burning" (Revelation 18:9).

We have been warned by the Word of God that in these last and evil days evil men and women would become worse and worse. It will become so bad that they will become deceitful and will deceive others just to get ahead. Mankind will sell out to Satan to obtain power.

<u>Lying wonders</u>,

> "even him, whose coming is after the working of Satan with all power and lying wonders" (2 Thessalonians 2:9).

According to the book of Revelation, during the tribulation period after the saints of the Lord have been caught up to heaven Satan will use great wonders to deceive those that still dwell on the earth. These wonders include such things as fire coming down from heaven (Revelation 13:13), and the beast or dragon being mortally wounded able to rise from the dead (Revelation 13:3). With lying wonders like these it is no wonder people will want to worship the dragon because they will think he is God.

<u>Demon of oppression</u>,

> "He was oppressed, and he was afflicted, yet he opened not his mouth" (Isaiah 53:7a).

It was foretold in the book of Isaiah (Isaiah 53:1) that Jesus was oppressed by the devil. When we read the fulfillment of this prophecy in the New Testament we see how Jesus was lied on, beaten, ridiculed, hated, scorned, and over powered, but in all this Jesus did not open his mouth to complain, because He knew what his mission was and He knew that the demons would come against him to stop him from fulfilling God's plan if they could.

and

"How God anointed Jesus of Nazareth with the Holy Ghost and with power: who went about doing good, and healing all that were oppressed of the devil, for God was with him" (Acts 10:38).

When Jesus was baptized in the Jordon River by John the Baptist, God manifested Himself in the trinity that He is. (1) God the Father speaking from heaven to His (2) Son, Jesus, and (3) the Holy Spirit descending upon Jesus like a dove. Jesus was empowered or anointed by His Father God to go about doing good, laying hands on the sick, casting out devils that had oppressed people, raising the dead, and doing what His Father had sent him to do.

Edith P. Lazenby

Demon of Divination,

"There shall not be found among you any one that maketh his son or his daughter to pass through the fire, or that useth divination, or an observer of times, or an enchanter, or a witch," Or a charmer, or a consulter with familiar spirits, or a wizard, or a necro- mancer" (Deuteronomy 18:10-11).

"And it came to pass, as we went to prayer, a certain damsel possessed with a spirit of divination met us, which brought her masters much gain by soothsaying:" (Acts 16:16).

We think nothing about going to the tea readers, psyches, root workers, astrologers, witches and any other followers of Satan to have our "future" told. It starts out so very innocent, until one wonders, well they told me this or that and they were right on the mark. Yes, the person that was consulted through the occult had or has a familiar spirit that knows everything about you. Once you believe or fall prey to this type of demonic influence you open yourself to be demon possessed or oppressed. The soothsayer is a person that supposedly tells the future for a fee. We all want to know the future, but all we have to do is read the Word of God, the Bible and we will know the future.

<u>Familiar Spirit,</u>

> "And the soul that turneth after such as having familiar spirits, and after wizards, to go a whoring after them, I will even set my face against that soul, and will cut him off from among his people" (Leviticus 20:6).

> "And he made his son pass through the fire, and observed times, and used enchantments, and dealt with familiar spirits and wizards: he wrought much wickedness in the sight of the Lord, to provoke him to anger" (2 Kings 21:6).

> "Then said Saul, unto his servants, seek me a woman that have a familiar spirit, that I may go to her, and enquire of her. And his servants said to him, behold, there is a woman that hath a familiar spirit at Endor" (1 Samuel 28:7).

A familiar spirit as mentioned above is a demon that has been assigned to you and know all about your past, the people in your family and people you know, so when a spiritualist or psyche supposedly tells you things you already know they are getting this information from a familiar spirit. This spirit is trying to take the place of God, and God has said in the first commandment, "thou shall no other gods besides me." We have to look to God for the answers to our problems and not to people who have a familiar spirit also known as a demon.

The Spirit of Heaviness,

> "To appoint unto them that mourn in Zion, to give unto them beauty for ashes, the oil of joy for mourn- ing, the garment of praise for the spirit of heaviness:" (Isaiah 61:3).

I would like to say this about the spirit of heaviness. This spirit descends on us if we let it when we lose someone very close to us, and we don't know how to accept death as a part of life. I know it's natural to have a period of mourning, but it's not natural for us to go into a period of depression, whereby we neglect ourselves, shut out everything, refuse to seek help, and waste away.

This is one area we have to conquer on our own and if not it will conquer us. In some places people are told not to cry, because you are a man, and men don't cry. This is a big fallacy. Crying help alleviate pent up emotions that need to get out. Not only that but the spirit of heaviness leads to other things such as self pity, broken relationships, and if a person is not really strong enough to pull themselves out of this state it may eventually lead to suicide.

<u>Demon or Spirit of Fear</u>,

> "For God hath not given us a spirit of fear; but of power, and of love and of a sound mind" (2 Timothy 1:7).

> "There is no fear in love; but perfect love casteth our fear: because fear hath torment. He that feareth is not made perfect in love" (1 John 4:18).

We are not fearful people, but things happen in our lives that make us fearful. Once we entertain this spirit it is hard to get rid of it until it is cast out by the love of God. Fear causes us to be afraid even of our own shadow. Each of us holds the key to our destiny. Love God, or love the devil. Love and serve God, and be delivered from the spirits and torments of Satan. Love God and abide in him and He will give you divine protection from the enemy whereas you will have nothing to fear.

Demon or Spirit of Infirmity,

> "And, behold, there was a woman which had a spirit of infirmity eighteen years, and was bowed together, and could in no wise lift up herself. And when Jesus saw her, he called her to him, and said unto her, woman, thou art loosed from thine infirmity. And he laid his hands on her: and immediately she was made straight, and glorified God" (Luke 13:11-13).

We need to realize that the sickness we deal with are not from God, but from Satan. He doesn't mind if you suffer because he knows what his fate is and he seems to enjoy inflicting God's creation with crippling diseases which are caused by the spirit of infirmity. Since we have never been taught how to deal with these spirits when they come against us, we become bound by them. If the Holy Spirit resides in us then we have the privilege of casting out these spirits. Satan's job is to destroy you and then get you to blame God for putting these things on you. It's not God's doing but that of Satan.

Demon of Sorcery,

"And I will come near to you to judgment: and I will be a swift witness against the sorcerers, and against the adulterers, and against false swearers, and against those that oppress the hireling in his wages, the widow, and the fatherless, and that turn aside the stranger from his right, and fear not me, saith the Lord of hosts" (Malachi 3:5).

"But the fearful, and unbelieving, and the abominable, and murderers, and whoremongers, and sorcerers, and idolaters, and all liars, shall have their part in the lake which burneth with fire and brimstone: which is the second death" (Revelation 21:8).

Sorcery is "the supposed use of an evil supernatural power over people and their affairs:

witchcraft; black magic."[3] This type of person is frowned upon by God, and his children should not like or support what God does not like or support. There is coming a time when God will judge people who deal in the supernatural to bring about bondage, sickness, oppression and other ungodly acts of Satan.

Spirit of anti-christ,

> "And every spirit that confesseth not that Jesus Christ is come in the flesh is not of God: and this is that spirit of anti-christ, whereof ye have heard that it should come, and even now already is it in the world" (1 John 4:3).

> "Little children, it is the last time and as ye have heard that antichrist shall come, even now are there many anti-christs; where by we know that it is the last time:" (1 John 2:18).

We have numerous cults throughout the world that deny the deity of Jesus Christ. Every

---

[3] Webster's New World Dictionary of the American Language, College Edition, The World Publishing Company, Cleveland and New York, 1966, p.1391.

human being that is born has a soul and a spirit. A outer man (soul) and an inner man (spirit), which wants to worship something or someone. When we are born into this world we are legally separated from our Creator which is God. Since we are separated from God there is only one other force we can be attached to and that is Satan. The Word of God states in Psalm 51:5, "behold, I was shapened in iniquity; and in sin did my mother conceive me." We are given a choice to either believe or accept Jesus has come in the flesh and died to forgive us of our sins, or we can believe this is nothing but a trick of the enemy to believe a lie. We have to make a choice to either believe the Word of God or the lies of Satan. We are either for Christ or anti-christ.

Unclean Spirit,

"For he said unto him, Come out of the man, thou unclean spirit" (Mark 5:8).

"And when he had called unto him his disciples, he gave them power against unclean spirits, to cast them out, and to heal all manner of sickness and all manner of disease" (Matthew 10:1).

Any spirit that is not of God is an unclean spirit. Any spirit that causes you to use profanity and do unseeingly things is an unclean spirit. Any spirit that prevents a normal person to be clean, to take care of their body is an unclean spirit. Any spirit that causes sickness and disease is an unclean spirit.

These are just some of the demonic spirits that the Word of God speaks about, to let us know that demons are real, and they can inhabit people and bind people and keep them in bondage.

~Jobs of Angels~

First let us look at the job of the fallen angels now known as demons. In the book of Daniel we find a very interesting story. It is the answer to why some of our prayers are not answered. Daniel prayed to God, but the answer to his prayer did not come until 21 days had past. Daniel did all he could by fasting and praying while waiting for God to answer his prayer. Sometimes when we pray and God doesn't answer our prayer as fast as we would like, we want to give up and figure God didn't hear us. It's not that God didn't hear us; it's that the answer to our prayers was held up by demons.

Daniel learned the reason his prayer had taken so long to be answered was when the angel came to him and said, God heard your prayer, but the demon that was assigned over the kingdom of Persia hindered me and Michael the archangel came to give me a hand, and he is still fighting, so I must go back and join him. Even though we are unable to see demons or angels with our natural eyes unless they are opened by God, they control the atmosphere, because the Bible says Satan is the "prince of the air." So we see that it is the job of the fallen angels to hinder the prayers of the saints.

> "Then said he unto me, Fear not, Daniel: for from the first day that thou didst set thine heart to understand, and to chasten thyself before thy God, thy words were heard, and I am come for thy word. But the prince of the kingdom of Persia withstood me one and twenty days; but, lo, Michael, one of the chief princes, came to help me; and I remained there with the kings of Persia" (Daniel 10:12-13).

This one verse of scripture tells us there are territorial demons. Since Satan was expelled from heaven he became the prince of this world, which gives him and his angels rule in certain areas. This also lets us know why some areas seems to be prospering while other areas seems to be run down, in disarray, full of drugs, prostitution, and all sorts of evil. I realize this is hard to believe, but once again we must go to the scriptures to verify this. When Jesus crossed over the Sea of Galilee to the other side,

> "And when he was come to the other side into the country of the Gergesenes, there met him two possessed with devils, coming out of the tombs, exceeding fierce, so that no man might pass by that way" (Matthew 8:28).

Mark 5:1-3 states it this way:

> "And they came over unto the other side of the sea, into the country of the Gadarenes. And when he was come out of the ship, immediately there met him out of the tombs a man with an unclean spirit, who had his dwelling among the tombs; and no man could bind him, no, not with chains."

People who are demon possessed exhibit strength which no normal human can exhibit. But they must come under subjection to the Holy Spirit. People fail to realize there are two worlds that exist, a natural world and a spiritual world, and we live in both these worlds whether we want to admit it or not. We cannot see everything with the naked eye, but we can see when someone is in their natural state or right mind. You can feel the oppression of evil spirits when you are filled with the Holy Spirit, because the Bible states, to try the spirit by the spirit.

We as children of God do not have to accept the sickness and diseases that Satan and his angels try to inflict us with. We must use the Word of God against him and plead the blood of Jesus.

> "They overcame him by the blood of the Lamb, and by the word of their testimony; and they loved not their lives unto death" (Revelation 12:11).

This is easy to say, but hard to do. I say this because when sickness or disease comes upon us we forget everything the Bible taught us, and we run to the medical doctor instead of running to God. This is natural because we live in a natural world and we are accustomed to doing natural things. When we come to our senses and realize it is God we should be turning to results start to happen. Don't get me wrong, there is nothing wrong with doctors. They are put here to help us, because everyone does not believe in divine healing from God. Even Jesus had a physician numbered among the twelve disciples. What we need to do is arm ourselves with the armor of God as found in Ephesians 6:13-18 which states:

> "Wherefore take unto you the whole armor of God, that ye may be able to withstand in the evil day, and having done all, to stand. Stand therefore, having your loins gird about with truth, and having on the breastplate of righteousness; And your feet shod with the preparation of the gospel of peace; Above all, taking the shield of faith, wherewith ye shall be able to quench all the fiery darts of the wicked. And take the helmet of salvation, and the sword of the Spirit, which is the word of God: Praying always with all prayer and supplication in the Spirit, and watching thereto with all perseverance and supplication for all saints."

So what does all this mean? To use as an analogy, let's take a boxer for example. He is going to train for the upcoming fight. He is going to study his opponent, watch his moves, look for his weak points, and practice his own technique, because he seems to know what he is up against. He is going to train, train, train and train some more.

We have been given a training manual whereby we can study so when our enemy, Satan comes against us, we will know how to fight against these demonic angels. Why do I say demonic beings? Let's step back a moment to the Old Testament book of Job where we read:

> "Then Satan answered the Lord, and said, Doth Job fear God for nought?..... And the Lord said unto Satan, Behold, all that he hath is in thy power; only upon himself put not forth thine hand. So Satan went forth from the presence of the Lord" (Job 1:9; 12).

So we see it is not God that put sickness upon us, it is Satan. Satan had to come before God to get permission to afflict Job and he has to get permission from God to persecute or afflict you with sickness or destruction of your possessions. God allows this as a test to what you have said, so we need to be careful of the words we speak, because not only does God hear us, but Satan also hears us, and he accuses us before God day and night. Yes, we are going to be tested as to who our allegiance belongs to. Is it God or Satan? We will be tested to see if our words are true, or if our words are just empty words when something drastic happens to us.

What is truth? God's Word is truth. He has given us His Word to fight against the wiles of the devil. What words are you talking about? I'm talking about the Bible. We find numerous scriptures that tell us "I am the Lord that healeth thee" (Exodus 15:26), "Many are the afflictions of the righteous: but the Lord delivereth him out of them all" (Psalm 34:19), "He sent his word, and healed them" (Psalm 107:20), "with his stripes we are healed" (Isaiah 53:5). These and many other scriptures throughout the Bible lets us know it is not God's will that we are sick or that we are attacked by diseases.

However, when we look at chapter 28 in the Old Testament book of Deuteronomy we notice there are some conditions we must meet to be spared the chastisement of the Lord. Now I am not saying God put these things on you, but because of our disobedience to his Word He allows us to be afflicted by Satan and his angels. The word states, "having done all, to stand"(Ephesians 6:13), in these last and evil days.

As we look around us we see we are definitely living in an evil day. It seems demonic angels have been unleashed like never before. We never had the things that are happening today happen before. Whoever heard of mass killings of innocent children just because someone felt like killing children? Whoever heard of children plotting to kill their mother and father, their siblings, and even their classmates because they were tired of taking orders and living? Who ever heard of arming yourself and killing innocent people in the name of the god you serve? Granted, there is nothing new under the sun, but things like the ones listed above was never carried out to the extent things are happening today. There are some things we as individuals must do today if we want to keep our sanity and they are:

(1) Believe and stand on the Word of God.
(2) Have faith in the Word of God.
(3) Pray and fast and ask God for his divine protection.
(4) Praise God, because as the saying goes, "when praises go up blessings come down."
(5) Keep the faith and hold on to God, no matter what the circumstances are.

(6) Believe God. What He has said, He will surely bring it to pass.

We have to submit ourselves to the will of God and the devil will flee from you. "Submit yourselves therefore to God. Resist the devil, and he will flee from you" (James 4:7), "because your adversary the devil, as a roaring lion, walketh about, seeking whom he may devour" (1 Peter 5:8). So how does a person submit themselves to God? Psalm 119:11 states;

> "Thy word have I hid in my heart,
> that I might not sin against thee."

and

> "Thy word is a lamp unto my feet,
> and a light unto my path" (Psalm
> 119:105).

The secret or prescription is to study God's Word daily. When we study and meditate on the Word of God, we have a mighty weapon to use against the enemy. Once we get His Word in our heart we will know what sin is and what is not sin. Anything that knowingly goes against the Word of God is sin, and Satan and his angels knows this, therefore they are constantly tempting you to go against the things of God. What looks good and sounds good is not always good that is why it is always good to try the spirit by the spirit.

> "Beloved, believe not every spirit, but try the spirits whether they are of God: because many false prophets are gone out into the world." (1 John 4:1).

We must be alert at all times against the devil, because "the devil, as a roaring lion, walketh about, seeking whom he may devour" (1 Peter 5:8). He is very subtle and he will use anyone he can to bring you down. Don't forget Satan is known or was known as an angel of light. He knows all the ropes, your weaknesses, your temptations, your likes and dislikes, and he will use this information against you. This is why it is so important to stay tuned into God, read his Word and most of all pray.

Matthew 16:19 states;

> "And I will give unto thee the keys of the kingdom of heaven: and whatsoever thou shalt bind on earth shall be bound in heaven: and whatsoever thou shalt loose on earth shall be loosed in heaven."

What does this mean? Let's take a look a moment at heaven. Revelation 21:4 states;

> "And God shall wipe away all tears from their eyes; and there shall be no more death, neither sorrow, nor crying, neither shall there be any more pain: for the former things are passed away."

A perfect environment will once again exist where everything is pure. When Jesus left heaven and came to earth he left a perfect environment and entered a world filled with suffering, disease, death, poverty and everything that is against a perfect environment. We must remember it wasn't always this way when God created the universe. He created a perfect environment. An environment without any form of corruption and sin. God made a perfect garden, and two perfect people whom he placed in the perfect environment to keep and to take care of with just one restriction; do not eat from the tree of the knowledge of good and evil. Funny how when we are told not to do something our antenna of curiosity goes up and we wonder; am I really being told the truth about why? What's going to really happen if I do what I'm told not to do?

That's what happened in the Garden of Eden. But prior to this incident occurring, Lucifer was expelled or as we like to say kicked out of heaven because he wanted to be God. He was created by God and he wanted to be God to be worshipped as God was being worshipped by the angels he had created. But God is God and he will not share his glory with another. Earth became corrupt because of the pronouncement of God upon it. Man would now have to live by the sweat of his brow. No longer could he walk about in a perfect environment, reach up and pick any kind of fruit he wanted off a tree to eat, now in order to eat he would have to plant, water, and tend to his plantings.

Mankind ruined a perfect thing when he disobeyed God, and listened to another voice. Today Christians need to be cognizant that there are more than one voice in the world. They are the voice of God, the voice of Satan, and the voice of self. Plenty times the voice of self overrules the voice of both God and Satan and then when things go awry we blame either God or Satan for what we decided we wanted to do.

Although angels are angelic beings and are considered to be spirits they have often appeared to men in visible form. An example of this can be found in Genesis chapter 19 when two angels visited Sodom to warn Lot to flee with his family, because God was going to destroy the city (Genesis 19:1). The sin of the people had come up before God, but Abram, Lot's uncle had interceded with the angel that had appeared to him (Genesis 19:20-33), for the Lord to spare the city if 10 righteous people could be found in the city. Unfortunately there was not ten righteous people, but because of Abram, Lot's uncle, Lot, and his two daughters were spared from the destruction that God rained down on Sodom and Gomorrah and the surrounding cities, because their gross sin in the face of God.

> "And their came two angels to Sodom at even; and Lot sat in the gate of Sodom: and Lot seeing them rose up to meet them; and he bowed himself with his face to the ground" (Genesis 19:1).

The world is facing some of the same problems that existed in Sodom during the time of Lot. Sodomy was running rampart and the men of Sodom wanted to seduce any male that came

Edith P. Lazenby

to their city. The whole city was corrupt. From the judicial system all the way down to the religious system. It should be noted that angels always appeared in masculine form, never in feminine form. One example of divine protection by a heavenly host of angels occurred when the king of Syria sent his men to capture or as the Bible states, to fetch Elisha, and bring him to the king. Then Elisha's young servant saw that the city was compassed about by chariots and horses and quite naturally he was afraid and alarmed. God always protects his servants and Elisha's response to his servant was by prayer when he prayed to the Lord.

> "Lord, I pray thee, open his eyes that he may see. And the Lord opened the eyes of the young man; and he saw: and, behold, the mountain was full of horses and chariots of fire round about Elisha" (2 Kings 6:17).

In Psalm 34:7 we find these comforting words,

> "the angel of the Lord, encampeth round about them that fear him, and delivereth them."

Psalm 34:7 in the Living Bible sums it up this way,

> "For the Angel of the Lord guards and rescues all who reverence him."[4] (Psalm 37:7) TLB.

Another time an angel appeared to man was to Gideon who called him "a mighty man of valor" (Judges 6:12). And when the angel Gabriel appeared unto Daniel to let him know his prayer was heard the first day he prayed, but he was hindered by the Prince of Persia (Daniel 10:13). When Balak was told by Baalam to curse the Israelites and an angel with a flaming sword stood in the way to stop the donkey that was carrying Balak to pass (Numbers 22:22-27).

Well, you say that was in the Old Testament. Well, in the New Testament angels are noted in John 20:12 which states:

> "And seeth two angels in white sitting, the one at the head, and the

---

[4] The Living Bible Paraphrased, Special Crusade Edition for the Billy Graham Evangelistic Association, (Minneapolis, Minnesota), 1972, p.456.

other at the feet, where the body of
Jesus had lain."

Another time while Jesus is on the Mount of
Olives giving his last instructions to his disciples,
before his ascension.

> "Ye men of Galilee, why stand ye
> gazing up into heaven? this same
> Jesus, which is taken up from you
> into heaven, shall so come in like
> manner as ye have seen him go
> into heaven" (Acts 1:11).

Angels are sent to help the children or I
should say the saints of God. Take the case of the
three Hebrew boys who was thrown into a fiery
furnace. When the king looked in he saw four
men instead of three, and the king said the fourth
one looks just like the Son of God. How did the
king know this? He knew this because he is also a
spiritual being. God himself appeared as the angel
of the Lord to protect his children from harm.

> "Are they not all ministering
> spirits, sent forth to minister
> for them who shall be heirs of
> salvation?" (Hebrew 1:14).

When we are going through trials and tribulations angels are sent to encourage the child of God. Let's take a look in Acts 27:23-24 when the angel of God came to Paul to encourage him in time of distress aboard a ship in a storm.

> "For there stood by me this night the angel of God, whose I am, and whom I serve, saying, fear not, Paul; thou must be brought before Caesar: and, lo, God hath given thee all them that sail with thee."

Of course the people did not believe Paul, because he was a prisoner they figured he did not know what he was talking about. Many people even in this day and age have visitations from angels. Some people see the angels and some people don't see them, but they can feel their presence. When God has a work for you to do, no devil in hell can stop you. He might impede you, delay you, but he cannot stop you.

~&Seraphims and Cherubims&~

The Word of God only speaks of seraphims twice and possibly three times and of Cherubims numerous times, but each play an important part in God's purpose. They are created to give godly reverence to God, and proclaim God's holiness. In Isaiah 6:2-3 and Isaiah 6:6, it states:

> "Above it stood the seraphims: each one had six wings; with twain he covered his face, and with twain he covered his feet, and with twain he did fly. And one cried unto another, and said, Holy, holy, holy, is the Lord of hosts; the whole earth is full of his glory" (Isaiah 6:2-3).

and

> "Then flew one of the seraphims unto me, having a live coal in his hand, which he had taken with the tongs from off the altar:" (Isaiah 6:6).

The other scripture which possibly refers to Seraphims can be found in Ezekiel chapter one.

The heavenly ministries of the mighty cherubim's are always connected with the throne of God. We first read of their ministry on earth when they were placed at the entrance of the Garden of Eden to prevent Adam and Eve from reentering the garden and possibly eating from the tree of life.

> "So he drove out the man; and he placed at the east of the garden of Eden Cherubims, and a flaming sword which turned every way, to keep the way of the tree of life" (Genesis 3:24).

Another instance where Cherubims are mention is in the wilderness tabernacle in the Holy of Holies, where the Ark of the Covenant was placed. We see that the cherubim's were made of gold and placed on either side overlooking the Mercy Seat. The mercy seat was a type of Christ, and the Cherubim's were overlooking the work of the Lord in love and light.

> "And thou shalt make two cherubims of gold, of beaten work shalt thou make them, in the two ends of the mercy seat. And make one cherub on the one end: and the other cherub on the other end; even of the mercy seat shall ye

make the cherubims on the two
ends thereof. And the cherubims
shall stretch forth their wings on
high, covering the mercy seat with
their wings, and their faces shall
look one to another, toward the
mercy seat shall thy faces of the
cherubims be" (Exodus 25:18-20).

Also, in Ezekiel 10:5 we find another
instance where the cherubims seem to represent
God himself.

"And the sound of the cherubims
wings was heard even to the outer
court, as the voice of the Almighty
God when he speaketh."

~❦Order of Angels❧~

The King James Version of the Bible only lists by name two archangels named Michael which means *who is as or like God*[5] and Gabriel which means *man or hero of God.*[6]

Archangels – Michael and Gabriel are the two archangels that are mentioned most in scripture. We first find the mention of Gabriel in the book of Daniel 8:16 when Gabriel was sent to explain the vision of the ram and he goat:

> "And I heard a man's voice between the banks of Ulai, which called, and said, Gabriel, make this man understand the vision."

Here we have one of the visions Daniel is given concerning the great tribulation which is to take place prior to the return of the Son of God. And another time Gabriel came to Daniel was when he was praying and petitioning God, for his people. Daniel 9:21-22 states,

---

[5] Ungers, Bible, p.728.

[6] Loc.cite. p.384.

"Yea, whiles I was speaking in prayer, even the man Gabriel, whom I had seen in the vision at the beginning, being caused to fly swiftly, touched me about the time of the evening oblation. And informed me, and talked with me, and said, O Daniel, I am now come forth to give thee skill and understanding."

The next time we encounter the angel Gabriel is when he appears to the priest named Zacharias, attending to his priestly duties to let him know that God has heard your prayers, and your wife Elizabeth is going to have a baby and she shall call his name John. Naturally Zacharias was surprised something like this was going to happen especially since his wife and him was well over the child bearing age. Luke 1: 19 states,

"And the angel answering said unto him, I am Gabriel, that stand in the presence of God; and am sent to speak unto thee, and to show thee these glad tidings" (Luke 1:19).

It appears that it is Gabriel that brings the message of good news to people because when

Elizabeth was six months pregnant he was sent to Nazareth to tell Mary she was going to have a baby and that her cousin Elizabeth was six months pregnant.

> "And in the sixth month the angel Gabriel was sent from God unto a city of Galilee, named Nazareth" (Luke 1:26).

The Bible also speaks of the archangel Michael in several places such as in Daniel 10:13 when Daniel had prayed about a dream he had had, and he petitioned the Lord for an understanding of his prayer;

> "But the prince of the kingdom of Persia withstood me one and twenty days: but, lo, Michael, one of the chief princes, came to help me; and I remained there with the kings of Persia" (Daniel 10:13).

This passage clearly explains why Daniel did not receive an answer to his prayer when he first prayed to God for the understanding of a vision he was given. It was held up by demonic beings in the atmosphere who hindered the answer from being delivered to Daniel for 21 days. In this passage Michael is described as "one of the chief princes." So here we see there are territorial demons. In Daniel 12:1 another mention of the archangel Michael is noted and it appears this time during the great tribulation which states;

> "And at that time shall Michael stand up, the great prince which standeth for the children of thy people: and there shall be a time of trouble, such as never was since there was a nation even to that same time: and at that time thy people shall be delivered, every one that shall be found written in the book."

It seems that the archangel Michael assignment is to protect the children of Israel. This is future and I believe during the time of the great tribulation, when all nations comes against God's chosen people. One other reference to the archangel Michael is in Jude verse 9 which states,

> "Yet Michael the archangel, when contending with the devil, he disputed about the body of Moses, durst not bring against him a railing accusation, but said, The Lord rebuke thee" (Jude vs 9).

Additionally, in the order of angels we have seraphims, cherubims, thrones, dominations or dominions, virtures, powers, principalities or princedoms, archangels and angels. An example of powers can be found in Ephesians 3:10 which states;

> "To the intent that now unto the principalities and powers in heavenly places might be known by the church the manifold wisdom of God."

An example of dominion or dominations can be found in Ephesians 1:20-21 which states,

> "Which he wrought in Christ, when he raised him from the dead, and set him at his own right hand in heavenly places, far above all principality, and power, and might, and dominion, and every name that is named, not only in this world, but also in that which is to come."

The order of angels can be summed up in Colossians 1:16 which states,

> "For by him were all things created, that are in heaven, and

that are in earth, visible and invisible, whether they be thrones, or dominions, or principalities, or powers: all things were created by him, and for him."

~Number of Angels~

The number of angels are innumerable for we see in Hebrews 12:22 it states,

> "But ye are come unto mount Sion, and unto the city of the living God, the heavenly Jerusalem, and to an innumerable company of angels."

Also in Revelation 5:11 we read,

> "And I beheld, and I heard the voice of many angels round about the throne and the beasts and the elders: and the number of them was ten thousand times ten thousand, and thousands of thousands."

Even Jesus states in Matthew 26:53,

> "Thinkest thou that I cannot now pray to my Father, and he shall presently give me more than twelve legions of angels?"

Six thousand composed a legion, so the Lord could have called seventy two thousand angels to come to his aid if he desired help.

Edith P. Lazenby

In 2 Kings 6:17 the city where Elisha was, it was surrounded by the Syrian army to take Elisha captive. Elisha's servant was upset when he saw the host that had compassed the city, but Elisha told his servant in no uncertain terms, don't worry about that, because "they that be with us are more than they that be with them" (2 Kings 6:16). Elisha's servant didn't understand this, because he was looking at things in the natural sense, so Elisha prayed and said,

> "Lord, I pray thee, open his eyes, that he may see. And the Lord opened the eyes of the young man; and he saw: and, behold, the mountain was full of horses and chariots of fire round about Elisha" (2 Kings 6:17).

So the eyes of the young man was opened, and he was able to see in the supernatural instead of the natural.

~Unusual Occurrences of Angels~

The book of Genesis holds some interesting facts concerning unusual occurrences of angels. One of those occurrences happened in Genesis chapter 32 whereby Jacob took advantage of his twin brother Esau. Jacob was a person who liked to stay home and close to the family. Esau was just the opposite. He was an outdoors man. One day Esau came in from the outside feeling very faint and Jacob saw a chance to trick Esau into giving him his birthright. Almost ready to pass out Esau sold his birthright to Jacob for a bowl of red pottage. When Esau regained his strength he realized what he had done. Jacob also tricked his father, Isaac into believing he was Esau to get the blessing of the family, because the first born always received the first blessing.

Jacob had to flee for his life because his brother Esau vowed to kill Jacob after they buried their father who had died. So Jacob with the help of his mother left home. After 14 years Jacob decided he wanted to return home and set out towards the home he had left. He was told by his servants Esau his brother was coming to meet him. You know when you do something wrong it stays with you, until you make it right.

Jacob had a dream whereby he saw a ladder come down from heaven with angels descending and ascending back and forth. With dawn approaching the angel needed to depart, but Jacob was found to be wrestling with the angel and would not let go of the angel and wanted to be assured of the promise God had give him. Jacob was blessed by the angel, who touched him in his thigh and after he was touched he became a disabled person who would now walk the rest of his life with a limp. Genesis 32:31-32 describes it this way;

> "And as he passed over Penuel the sun rose upon him, and he halted upon his thigh. Therefore the children of Israel eat not of the sinew which shrank, which is upon the hollow of the thigh, unto this day: because he touched the hollow of Jacob's thigh in the sinew that shrank."

The Living Bible explains it this way making it easier to understand,

The sun rose as he started on, and
he was limping because of his hip.
(That is why the people of Israel
still do not eat the sciatic muscle
where it attached to the hip)"[7]
(Genesis 32:31-32) TLB.

Another unusual occurrence occurs in
Genesis 6:1-4 whereby it is thought that some of the
fallen angels of the Lord left their natural state and
co-habited with the daughters of men. The story as
related in Genesis 6:1-4 is as follows:

"And it came to pass, when men
began to multiply on the face of
the earth, and daughters were
born unto them, that the sons of
God saw the daughters of men that
they were fair; and they took them
wives of all which they chose. And
the Lord said, My spirit shall not
always strive with man, for that
he also is flesh: yet his days shall
be an hundred and twenty years.
There were giants in the earth in
those days; and also after that,
when the sons of God came in
unto the daughters of men, and
they bare children to them, the

---

[7] <u>Ibid</u>. The Living Bible, p.30.

same became mighty men which
were of old, men of renown."

One can only wonder were these giants
that co-mingled with the daughters of men fallen
angels. We can only surmise, this is true according
to the Word of God. However, the consensus seems
to think so, because why would God be so upset
with what was ensuing, because Genesis 6:5 states,

"And God saw that the wickedness
of man was great in the earth,
and that every imagination of the
thoughts of his heart was only evil
continually."

It is believed that the fallen angels were the
giants that were in the land, and that they mingled
with the daughters of the sons of God which is
totally against the laws of God. God was vexed that
he made man, because man's intentions were only
evil and God made up in his mind that he would
destroy man whom he had created, and this would
include the giants which were probably the fallen
angels who had co-habited with mankind.

Another time angels are spoken of is when
Abraham, pleaded with God to spare Sodom if
there were ten righteous souls. It is so sad when you

read this story realizing there was not ten righteous people in the city of Sodom whereby it would not be destroyed. But God in his righteousness sent an angel to warn Abraham's nephew Lot, to flee Sodom, because of its wickedness God was going to destroy the city. But you know, you can live in an atmosphere which is not uplifting, one filled with wickedness, perversion, sexual immorality, and if you stay in this atmosphere long enough you become comfortable. Lot was comfortable in the environment he was in, and the angel of the Lord had to make Lot and his family leave. Genesis chapter 19 tells the story of the perverness of Sodom where Lot was living:

> "And there came two angels to Sodom at even; and Lot sat in the gate of Sodom: and Lot seeing them rose up to meet them; and he bowed himself with his face toward the ground" (Genesis 19:1),

and

> "And when the morning arose, then the angels hastened Lot, saying, Arise, take thy wife, and thy two daughters, which are here; lest thou be consumed in

the iniquity of the city" (Genesis 19:15).

Another unusual occurrence of angels is when Daniel was thrown into the lion's den because he would not stop praying to his God. The king was tricked into making some sort of decree that no one should pray or petition any God or man for thirty days, and if they did so, then they should be cast into the den of lions. Daniel 6:7 states;

> "All the presidents of the kingdom, the governors, and the princes, the counsellors, and the captains, have consulted together to establish a royal statute, and to make a firm decree, that whosoever shall ask a petition of any God or man for thirty days, save of thee, O King, he shall be cast into the den of lions."

The enemy which is Satan has the power to plant thoughts in your mind, and if you are not aware he is able to do this you will think you are acting on your own thoughts.

It seems like angels only appeared to people in the Old Testament. But, no, you also find angels mentioned in the New Testament. There are many instances, where angels appeared to individuals in the New Testament such as when the angel Gabriel appears to Mary and tells her she is going to have a baby (Luke 1:31), but at the time of this visitation she was not yet married to Joseph her future husband. Joseph wanted to put his wife away, to save both him and her embarrassment, because he thought she had cheated on him. Sometimes it's hard to understand and accept the supernatural unless you personally get a visitation from the Lord through the means of an angel. As Joseph pondered the thought of putting Mary his espoused wife away an angel appeared unto him and said:

> "But while he thought on these things, behold, the angel of the Lord appeared unto him in a dream, saying, Joseph, thou son of David, fear not to take unto thee Mary thy wife: for that which is conceived in her is of the Holy Ghost" (Matthew 1:20).

Another instance was when an angel appeared to someone was when Gabriel, appeared unto a priest named Zacharias, as he was performing his priestly duties in the temple. The angel which was named Gabriel came to tell him that his wife Elizabeth, as old as she was, was going to have a baby and that his name was to be John (Luke 1:7-20). After numerous years of praying Zacharias prayer was finally going to be answered, but because of such a delay in answered prayer and because he was an old man as was his wife (Luke 1:18), Zacharias could not believe this was possible. Sometimes it pays not to question God or his timing because God who is omniscience is able to take the impossible and turn it into the possible. Zacharias's son was to be the front runner for the coming of the Lord.

More importantly angels appeared at the tomb of Jesus after he had risen early on the morning of the third day. The Bible states two women, Mary Magdalene and the other Mary came to the tomb to see the sepulcher (Matthew 28:1), but when they arrived the stone was rolled away and an angel descended from heaven to let the women know Jesus was not there, but he had risen. Matthew 28:2-3 states it this way:

> "And, behold, there was a great earthquake: for the angel of the Lord descended from heaven, and came and rolled back the stone from the door, and sat upon it. His

countenance was like lightning
and his raiment white as snow."

Mark Chapter 16 verses 4-5 states it this way:

"And when they looked, they saw
that the stone was rolled away: for
it was very great. And entering
into the sepulchre, they saw a
young man sitting on the right side,
clothed in a long white garment;
and they were affrighted."

And in Luke 24:1-4 states the appearance of
the angel is explained this way:

"Now upon the first day of the
week, very early in the morning,
they came unto the sepulchre,
bringing the spices which they had
prepared, and certain others with
them. And they found the stone
rolled away from the sepulchre.
And they entered in, and found
not the body of the Lord Jesus.
And it came to pass, as they were
much perplexed thereabout,
behold, two men stood by them in
shining garments."

It is not always the case that good angels
will manifest themselves because the evil angels

in the form of demons often manifest themselves
through the body and voice of the individual whom
they have invaded, such as an example given to us
in Mark 1:23-24 which states:

> "And there was in their synagogue
> a man with an unclean spirit; and
> he cried out, saying, Let us alone;
> what have we to do with thee, thou
> Jesus of Nazareth? art thou come
> to destroy us? I know thee who
> thou art, the Holy One of God."

This is one of the fallen angels crying out
because he recognizes who Jesus is, and he knows
that his days are numbered. This passage in Mark
shows us that unbelievers, and sinners, those who
do not have Christ in their life can be inhabited
by demonic beings otherwise known as fallen
angels. We cannot send demons to hell when we
minister to individuals who are demon possessed,
because it is not their time to be held in bondage.
To verify this, there was a man in the country of
the Gadarenes who was demon possessed. No one
could come near him, but when Jesus went there
the man with the demons, or you can say the demon
recognized who Jesus was and he ran to him and
worshipped him. Why do you ask this occurred?

Probably because the man was momentarily in his right mind when he first saw Jesus and knew it was only Jesus that could set him free. Or the demons in the man recognized Jesus, and knew they were going to be cast out of the man. Mark 5:6-14, describes it this way:

> "But when he saw Jesus afar off, he ran and worshipped him, And cried with a loud voice, and said, what have I to do with thee, Jesus, thou Son of the most High God? I adjure thee by God, that thou torment me not. For he said unto him, Come out of the man, thou unclean spirit. And he asked him, What is thy name? And he answered, saying, my name is Legion: for we are many. And he besought him much that he would not send them away out of the country."

So if Jesus did not send the demon's to hell neither can we before their time. Oh, I realize we would like to do this, but not now. There is coming a time when this will occur, but at the present we just have to be patient and wait on God's timing.

Another instance of angels appearing unto man is when Jesus was giving his final instructions to his disciples before he was taken up to glory, in a cloud,

> "And when he had spoken these things, while they beheld, he was taken up; and a cloud received him out of their sight. And while they looked steadfastly toward heaven as he went up, behold, two men stood by them in white apparel:" (Acts 1:9-10).

So we see Jesus was taken up into heaven with angels by his side. One day Jesus is coming back, but there won't be only two angels at his side, it will be with multiple angels with him.

> "Which also said, Ye men of Galilee, why stand ye gazing up into heaven? this same Jesus, which is taken up from you into heaven, shall so come in like manner as ye have seen him go into heaven" (Acts 1:11).

> "For the Lord himself shall descend from heaven with a shout, with the voice of the archangel, and with the trump of God: and

the dead in Christ shall rise first:"
(1 Thessalonians 4:16).

The angels of the Lord proclaimed Jesus's birth by announcing it to the shepherds who were tending their sheep. Jesus was ministered to by angels (Matthew 4:11), after being tempted by Satan when he came off his wilderness fast. After Jesus was crucified and placed in a borrowed tomb the Word of God tells us, he went down to hell and set the captives free from the devil. On the third day two angels rolled the stone away from the grave where Jesus was laid. Jesus was seen on earth in his risen state for forty days. On the fortieth day Jesus was taken up into heaven, while his disciples watched him taken up. They were so transfixed on his departure from the Mount of Olives that the two angels that were there brought them back to reality by saying, why are you standing here, gazing up into heaven? The same way he was taken up into heaven he shall also return in like manner.

Two angels were there when Jesus the Son of God was taken up into heaven, but when Jesus returns for his bride, the archangel will make the announcement with a loud shout and with the trump of God. It will be a sound that even the dead will hear and they will rise first to join Jesus and the angels that accompany him in the air followed by the followers of Jesus who is alive, who will be changed from a mortal body to an immortal body.

～My Testimony About Angels～

In the beginning of this book I asked a question. Do you believe in angels? Are there good angels as well as bad angels? I would like to answer yes to both of these questions and share some background experience with you. I would first like to share my experience with the bad angels. You know you can read about things, but until you experience them for yourself they don't seem real. My first encounter with demons (fallen angels) was when I gave my life to Jesus and decided to divorce Satan, because all he could offer me was eternal life in a place called hell which burns constantly with fire and brimstone.

I had returned home from attending my church in Jamaica, Queens, to Bayshore where I was living. I prepared myself as happy as I could be for bed. Went to sleep and had the most terrifying experience of my life. A demon whom I believe to this day was Satan himself climbed on my bed I believe with the intent to destroy me. I have never seen something so grotesque and horrible in my life. All I could do was lie in the bed (mind you this was taking place in the spirit realm), and all I could do was call on the name of Jesus, and I was rescued from this awful thing. My fellow readers, Satan is real and his demons are real also.

Another time I saw a fallen angel manifest itself in a person, was when I accompanied Evangelist Joycelyn Bright (she has since been elevated to an Elder), to a deliverance service where she was ministering, and after the preaching an altar call was given for prayer. This one lady in the congregation started swaying and writhing like a snake. The pastor of the church ran from this demonic demonstration or manifestation, so that left Evangelist Bright and myself to deal with this demon. The Word of God tells us, "this kind only comes out by prayer and fasting." I am glad I was obedient and had prayed and fasted prior to attending this service with Evangelist Bright.

I will only give one more of my encounters with demons. We were ministering in Trinidad, West Indies on a crusade. This particular afternoon the Evangelist that was ministering, along with us was in a car on our way to where the crusade was being held. It had been raining, so naturally the streets were wet. The driver of the car informed us that the tires on her car were bald, so for us to pray that we would get to the crusade safely. No sooner had she said this we noticed at the intersection ahead of us was two cars partially blocking the intersection and there was no way humanly possible for us to get through them and we could not stop in time. Four of us were in the car and we all called on the name of Jesus at the same time. To this day, I don't know how we got through that little space, but I believe the angel of the Lord was there and he heard our cry. I give all praise, glory and honor to the Lord for the things he has done and has allowed me to share with you.

I do not want to continue talking about demonic beings, but I now want to share with you about the good angels. There have been numerous times when it felt like I was being touched by someone and when I looked around no one was there. This happened many times when I was growing up, but now since I am an adult it doesn't happen as often.

There have been times I put my car keys and house keys down and went back to pick them up so I could go to the store or take care of some necessary business. When I returned to get the keys they had disappeared without a sound. When this first happened to me I thought maybe I had placed the keys somewhere else besides where I normally place them. After an extensive search for the keys I gave up, went out the room to do something else, and when I returned to the room there was the keys. Was I losing it or what? No, I think the angels delayed me from going out when I wanted to and saved me from some impending danger.

There are two incidents that happened to me, and when I think about them it seems just like yesterday, because they are so vivid in my memory. I've testified numerous times to people so they will know that the Lord is real and he is no respecter of persons. The first incident occurred one night when I was on my way home from work. It had been snowing lightly and the temperature was below freezing. I didn't know anything about the term of black ice, back in 1976. I was on the Southern State Parkway driving at what I thought was a descent speed and other cars were doing the same. I came to a sharp curve and applied my brakes to further slow down. The car which I was driving was a blue Pontiac Tempest with a blacktop that started to skid and go into a spin. Mind you, there were cars next to me. I heard a loud bang and I just knew I was hit, and somehow I was able to get off to the side of the road. The other cars did not stop they just kept going. When I heard the loud bang all I did was call on the name of Jesus.

When I brought the car under control and gained my composure, because this was a frightening experience, I got out of the car to see how bad the damage was. I walked around the car twice, and I did not see any damage anywhere. I could hardly believe my eyes, considering it was dark. All I could say was thank you Jesus. I believe he sent his divine angel of protection at that precise moment to save me from an accident and it was an angel that struck the car and not another car. I got control of myself, got back in the car and drove home to Queens. I told my mother (Mrs. Marjorie Lazenby who at this writing is with the Lord), what had happened because I had gotten home later than normal. I went to bed and went to sleep thanking God for his goodness and when I got up the following morning I went outside to look at the car, and nothing was wrong with the car; no dents, nothing. I am so grateful to God for sending his protective angel to protect me that night, that I often tell people about this incident to let them know you can call on the name of Jesus and he'll be right there.

The second glorious and unbelievable incident occurred when my mother and I was headed to Washington, D.C., to attend my mother's sister's funeral. We had left Jamaica, New York the day before, because the weather was suppose to be coming up from the south and snow was headed our way. We stopped in Philadelphia, at my deceased aunt's house to rest. We got up early the next morning to continue on what we thought would be a 2 ½ hour trip. The further south we drove the worst the weather started to get.

I took the wrong exit and found a telephone to call my brother to let him know where we were and how to get to the funeral home because we were lost. I didn't have a cell phone at the time, but now I make sure I have a cell phone with me when I travel or just go out. Following the instructions my brother had given me my mother and I continued on our way at a snail's pace, because now the weather had really gotten worse; the roads were covered with ice and snow and the wind was blowing very hard. Traffic had slowed to a crawl, thank God for that, and as we (my mother and I), were going around this curve to get back on the parkway, the car started to slide, and then spin out. There was a ravine on our right side, cars behind us, snow and ice on the road before us, and we started to slide towards the ravine. All I could do was call on the name of Jesus three times. God sent his angel, I said God sent his angel and saved us from going into that ravine. I know God is real, and his angels are real. I wouldn't be here today, if God had not intervened in this harrowing situation. It's like the car was lifted and placed back on the road, and the cars behind us had stopped. To this day I believe an angel had stopped those cars. My mom and I saw the hand of God in our lives more than one time. The Word of God states, "the angel of the Lord encampeth round about them that fear him, and delivereth them." There are many more events that has happened in my life, so I know without a doubt God dispatches his angels when you call on the name of his Son, Jesus.

❧Judgment of Angels❧

What is the judgment of angels? Will they be saved? Is there any hope for these fallen angels? Unfortunately, there is no hope of redemption for the fallen angels, because in Jude verse 6 we find these words,

> "And the angels which kept not their first estate, but left their own habita-tion, he hath reserved in everlasting chains under darkness unto thejudgment of the great day."

Also, in 2 Peter 2:4 it states,

> "For if God spared not the angels that sinned, but cast them down to hell, and delivered them into chains of darkness to be reserved unto judgment."

And to further back up this statement Matthew 25:41 states;

> "Then shall he say also unto them on the left hand, depart from me, ye cursed, into everlasting fire, prepared for the devil and his angels."

The angels made their choice when they chose to follow and serve Satan, instead of serving and following their Creator, God. Just as the fallen angels and the angels in heaven made a choice, mankind has the opportunity to choose either to follow God, or God's adversary Satan. Once the choice has been made, and death finds you, you will either spend eternity in heaven with God, or in hell with Satan and the fallen angels from which there is no return. We cannot blame God for our final destination, because God has given us his Word the Bible to read. He has sent his only begotten Son, Jesus, to be the sacrificial Lamb to die in our place. God has sent prophets, teachers, films, and everything possible our way to show us the path we should walk in. With all the demonic type films and books that are in the market place today there is no mistake that Satan is real.

What he fails to tell you in these books and movies is that his place has been reserved in the lake of fire and brimstone, with unquenchable torment. Many turn a deaf ear to the gospel because they feel if they accept Christ as their savior then they will miss out on all the fun the world has to offer. Just the opposite is true. To accept and acknowledge Jesus in your life as your Lord and Savior is just the beginning of life. You gain life and not lose life.

The Word of God states, "and ye shall know the truth and the truth shall make you free" (John 8:32). Free from what you ask. Free from the bondage of sin. What is sin? Sin is everything that is against the will of God. Revelation 21:8 states,

> "But the fearful, and unbelieving, and the abominable, and murderers, and whoremongers, and sorcerers, and idolaters, and all liars, shall have their part in the lake which burneth with fire and brimstone: which is the second death."

Satan is constantly telling you everything that is mentioned in this particular verse of scripture is not true. Come on and have some fun. Live and be happy. Unfortunately, Satan, the adversary is lying to you, because he is the father of lies.

The good angels outweigh the bad angels, for in Psalm 23 we read, "goodness and mercy shall follow me all the days of my life." Sometimes

Edith P. Lazenby

when we get prepared to do something that is contrary to the will of God, we are stopped short by the angels that are assigned to us. How can I say this? Think for a moment, when you go someplace and see something you like, and realize you don't have enough money to buy the object, Satan will whisper in your ear, go ahead take it, or change the price tag, no one will ever know, but on the other hand you have the angel of mercy whispering in your ear, ask and see if they will mark the price down or put it on lay-a-way for you.

We do not need to yield to temptation when we are tempted. We need to take our rightful authority over Satan, and let him know, "it is written." Jesus over came temptation during his wilderness experience, and since we now belong to Jesus, though the blood of the Lamb that was slain on Calvary's cross, you too can overcome the temptation of Satan.

Yes, the fallen angels along with their leader, who was one of the most beautiful angel ever created made their decision where they will spend eternity. It is up to each individual who walks the face of this earth where they will spend eternity once there time on earth is completed. Will it be with God, or will it be with Satan? Will it be with the heavenly angels, or will it be with the fallen angels in the lake of fire? The choice is yours, for the Word of God states in Revelation 20:15,

> "And whosoever was not found written in the book of life was cast into the lake of fire."

～Summation～

The book of Revelation – which means the revealing of Jesus Christ – is filled with numerous connotations of angels of God doing God's bidding in these last and evil days. If you would read the book of Revelation – you will read about angels of God who are assigned to pour out judgments upon a disobedient people during the time of the tribulation period that is to come upon the world, who refuse to acknowledge God as God, and the preparation of the cleansing of the earth. This earth as we know it will pass away and a new heaven and a new earth will come down and replace the one we know.

To most people this sounds farfetched, a fairy tale, but God does not make a mistake and He does not lie. The adversary has distorted the Word of God so as to make it a mockery, and many people will not even read the Word of God; because if they do they will be held accountable for what they have read. But whether we read God's Word or not, we will still be held accountable for rejecting God, because we chose to serve the creature instead of the Creator.

Our eyes have been blinded to the truth and in our frailty we would rather accept a lie than the truth. Satan in his cunningness and craftiness has so distorted God's Word with these new Bibles on the market that allows people to do anything and everything contrary to His Word, and still make heaven their home. One day there is going to be a rude awakening for all who has followed the lies of Satan, and it will be too late.

From Genesis to Revelation, God has revealed truth to his people, but we don't want truth, because truth is like holding you captive. You cannot go out and have fun. You can have fun by serving God, because His word says, "the joy of the Lord is my strength." My testimony is I get joy when I think about what God has done for me. He saved my soul from the pit of hell, cleansed me up by the blood of the Lamb and placed my feet on solid ground, and gave me a peak at how the story ends. We who name the name of Jesus and serve him will one day go back to heaven with Jesus. Until that time comes we must run the race that is set before us, looking unto Jesus the Author and Finisher of our faith.

Angels and demons are real. Just like good and bad is real, or black and white is real. Heaven and hell are real. You cannot have one without the other. We have been put here to occupy until Jesus returns, and one day Jesus is coming back to gather his bride home, but as recorded in the Word of God the Bible before He comes back a great falling away will occur, which is happening today at an alarming rate, because people's eyes has been blinded by the adversary.

Angels are still being dispatched by God to protect his children, and demons are still attacking God's children, but one day all this will end. We will end up in our respective place dependent upon whom we have chosen to follow. God, which equates to heaven or hell which equates to the adversary known as Satan or the devil as used throughout this writing. The choice is yours.

As I close this book on "angels" I would like to offer you the reader the opportunity to repent of your sins, and choose Jesus as your Lord and savior. If you no longer want to serve the fallen angel Satan, or if you want to renew your commitment to Jesus, please bow you head and humble your heart as you repeat this simple prayer:

"Lord Jesus, forgive me of my sins, because I believe that I am lost without your Son, Jesus. I believe that you sent your only begotten Son, Jesus, to live, die, and rise again just for me, and one day He's coming back for me and I want to be ready when He comes. I believe Jesus is the Christ, the Son of the Living God, and I am asking you to come into my heart now, cleanse me from all unrighteousness, and I will live and serve you for the rest of my life. Thank you Jesus for saving me. Amen.

Bibliography

1. The Scofield Study Bible, King James Version, New York, Oxford World University Press, 1966.

2. The Living Bible Paraphrased, Special Crusade Edition for the Billy Graham Evangelistic Association, Minneapolis, Minnesota, 1972.

3. Unger, Merrill F., Unger's Bible Dictionary, Moody Press, Chicago, 1966.

4. Webster's New World Dictionary of the American Language, College Edition, The World Publishing Company, Cleveland and New York, 1966.